EARTH

eXtreme FACTS

BY STEFFI CAVELL-CLARKE

SECRET BOOK COMPANY

©2018
The Secret Book Company
King's Lynn
Norfolk PE30 4LS

ISBN: 978-1-912171-90-3

All rights reserved
Printed in Malaysia

Written by:
Steffi Cavell-Clarke
Edited by:
Kirsty Holmes
Designed by:
Jasmine Pointer

A catalogue record for this book
is available from the British Library

PHOTO CREDITS

Abbreviations: l-left, r-right, b-bottom, t-top, c-centre, m-middle.

CONTENTS

Words that look like <u>this</u> can be found in the glossary on page 24.

PLANET EARTH

Planet Earth is the only place in the solar system that we know supports life. We haven't found life anywhere else in the universe (yet!).

Our planet contains millions of different life forms which have <u>adapted</u> to Earth's diverse <u>environments</u>.

Earth provides many different habitats. A habitat is a place where an animal lives.

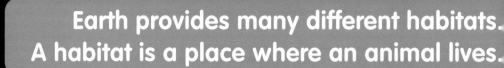

All living things need a habitat that provides the things they need to survive, such as water, air and sunlight.

Animals, plants and humans are all living things.

4

Earth's surface is covered in land and water.

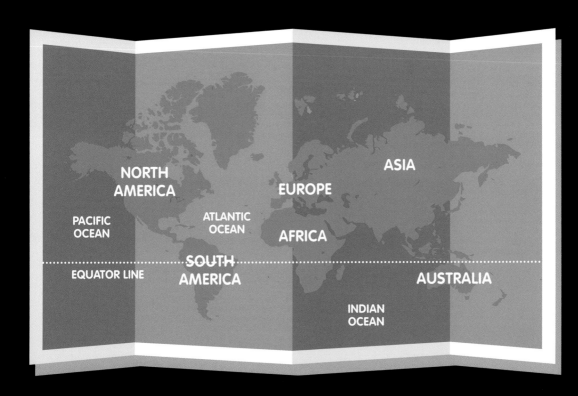

The land and water on the **Equator** has the hottest **climate,** whereas the polar regions experience freezing temperatures.

From the lush rainforests to the barren deserts, planet Earth has many different landscapes and environments to explore. Let's have a look!

OCEANS

An ocean is a very large area of salty sea water. The oceans are some of the most mysterious and unexplored part of the world.

There are rocks, sand, mud and seaweed on the ocean floor. Scientists believe that we have only explored 5% of it!

The ocean covers around 70% of the Earth's surface.

The oceans are constantly moving. Gravity and wind make waves that lap up on the shores and coastlines of the land.

Seawater is far too salty for humans to drink, yet millions and millions of animals thrive in the ocean water.

From tiny krill to great white sharks, animals have adapted to live in these watery environments in amazing ways.

The ocean is the world's biggest habitat, home to billions of fish and plant life.

The lowest point on Earth is in the Pacific Ocean, and is called the Challenger Deep. It is 10,994 meters (m) deep!

Fish were already living in the oceans long before dinosaurs evolved on land.

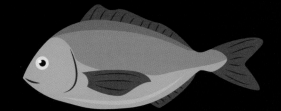

POLAR REGIONS

Planet Earth has two polar regions, which are the most northern and southern parts of the world.

They are the coldest parts of the planet. The temperature can fall below -40 degrees Celsius (°C) at the South Pole.

The lowest temperature measured at the South Pole was -82.8°C in 1982.

Covered in snow and ice, the polar regions are the harshest environments in the world.

The Arctic region is found at the northern-most part of the world. It is mostly made up of the frozen Arctic Ocean with very little land.

N

S

Antarctica is the region around the South Pole. It is a frozen, mountainous <u>continent</u> surrounded by the Southern Ocean.

Polar bears actually have black skin under their fur! Even more amazing is that the fur isn't white, it is <u>transparent</u>. It just looks white!

Not many animals can live and survive in Antarctica, apart from penguins, seals and albatrosses.

RAINFORESTS

Rainforests are forests with many trees that often experience heavy rainfall.

N

Equator

S

They grow throughout the tropical zone close to the Equator. It is normally warm and wet all year round. This helps the plants to grow and produce fruits and flowers.

The many trees and plants in the rainforests give out huge amounts of <u>oxygen</u>.

Almost all animals need oxygen to live, so it is very important to look after the Earth's rainforests.

The Amazon rainforest is the largest rainforest in the world.

From the treetops to the forest floor, rainforests are teeming with animal life, such as birds, snakes, jaguars, chameleons and monkeys.

The Kapok tree is the tallest tree that grows in the rainforest. It can grow to over 60 m!

Do you like chocolate?
The cocoa tree grows in tropical climates and can be found in the rainforest.

Scientists believe that there may be millions of plant and insect <u>species</u> in the rainforests that haven't been discovered yet.

DESERTS

A desert is a large area of land that has very little rainfall. It can be a very harsh environment, but many animals have adapted to survive there.

Deserts currently cover one-fifth of the Earth's surface. They can be found in all sorts of locations, from mountains to coasts – and even Antarctica!

The Sahara desert in Africa is believed to be the largest hot desert on Earth. It is home to many animals, such as baboons and hyenas.

Not many plants or animals can live in hot deserts, but those that do have adapted to help them to survive with very little water.

The cactus is a type of water storing plant found in desert regions. **Almost all types of cactus can only be found in North and South America.**

Many animals living in the deserts are nocturnal. This means that they sleep throughout the hot days and come out at night to hunt for <u>prey</u> when the temperature is cooler.

MOUNTAINS

Mountains are large areas of land made from rock and earth that rise above the Earth's surface.

The Earth's crust is made up of tectonic plates.
Many mountains were formed when the Earth's tectonic plates smashed into each other.

Mountains can be found on every continent and even beneath the ocean.

The highest mountain on Earth is Mount Everest, which is 8,848 m high.

Mountains usually have steep sides that are rocky and bare. Some mountains have trees growing on their sides too and very tall mountains often have snow on their peaks.

The mountain peaks have the coldest temperatures.

Mountain ranges are a large group of mountains next to each other.

The Andes are the longest mountain range on land in the world at 11,265 kilometres (km).

Mountains can also be found under the ocean! They are called **seamounts**.

VOLCANOES

Volcanoes are openings in the Earth's surface. They can be active, <u>dormant</u> or extinct.

When volcanoes are active, they could <u>erupt</u> and release ash, gas and hot magma.

Volcanic eruptions can send ash high up into the air, up to 30 km above the Earth's surface.

Hot liquid rock under the Earth's surface is known as magma. It is called lava after it comes out of a volcano.

Extinct volcanoes have not erupted in the past 10,000 years and are unlikely to erupt again.

They are often found at the meeting points of tectonic plates.

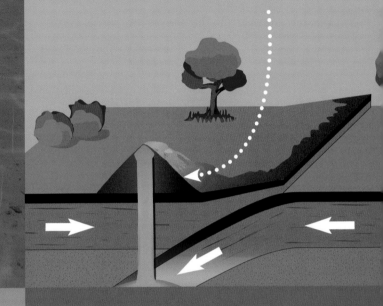

They are many volcanoes on Earth, both on land and at the bottom of the sea floor.

There are around 1,500 volcanoes that have erupted on land within the last 10,000 years.

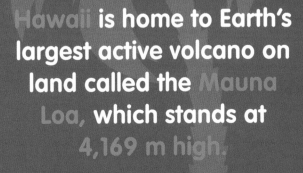

Hawaii is home to Earth's largest active volcano on land called the Mauna Loa, which stands at 4,169 m high.

RIVERS AND STREAMS

Much of Earth's landscape has been shaped by flowing rivers.

Rivers start as small streams. The <u>source</u> of the water may come from a <u>spring</u> on a hillside or even from a <u>glacier</u>.

The water trickles into a stream which flows quickly into a river.

Rivers, streams, lakes and ponds usually contain fresh water, which is different to the saltwater found in the ocean.

The longest river on Earth is the River Nile in Egypt. It reaches around 6,853 km long. ········➤

It is home to many different animals, such as crocodiles and turtles.

Many rivers around the world are <u>polluted</u> by rubbish. This is very harmful to the wildlife that lives in them. ········➤

Sometimes, the water is so dirty that it is very dangerous to swim in it or drink it.

TOWNS AND CITIES

Towns and cities are <u>urban</u> areas that have buildings such as houses, shops and schools.

The world is home to over seven billion humans. Over half of the world's human population now live in towns and cities

There are thousands of cities around the world. Many of them have tall skyscrapers. Some skyscrapers have tens of thousands of people living or working inside.

One of the largest cities in the world is Shanghai, which has over 24 million people living in it.

As towns and cities have grown in size and number, more and more of Earth's natural environments have either been destroyed or harmed.

HELPING THE EARTH

Earth is a unique planet. It is the only planet in the solar system that has the ideal conditions for living things to survive.

Humans have had a huge impact on the Earth's natural environments.

Millions of trees are cut down every year for <u>fuel</u>. This is destroying many habitats and leading to many species of animal becoming extinct.

Humans pollute the planet in many other ways that are damaging Earth's land, water and air.

You can make a difference! There are loads of ways that you can help the Earth and stop pollution.

Here are three easy ways that you can help to stop pollution:

Switch off lights when you leave a room.

Donate old clothes and shoes to charity.

Recycle your rubbish and buy foods with less packaging.

Remember, we only have one Earth, so we all need to take care of it!

GLOSSARY

adapted — changed over time to suit the environment

climate — the weather in a large area

continent — one of the world's main areas of land

dormant — slowed down for a period of time

environments — the surrounding areas

Equator — an imaginary line through the centre of the Earth

erupt — blast out of the ground

fuel — a material that is burned to produce heat or power

glacier — a slow-moving section of ice

gravity — a force that pulls towards the centre of the Earth

oxygen — a natural gas that all living things need in order to survive

polluted — contaminated with harmful substances

prey — animals that are hunted by other animals for food

source — where something starts or comes from

species — a group of very similar animals that are capable of producing young together

spring — where water flows from the Earth's surface

tectonic plates — sub-layers of the Earth's crust

transparent — a material that lets light pass through it, causing it to be see-through

urban — relating to a town or city

INDEX